It's Your Time

It's Your Time

SANDRA DONALD

To Di what can I say other than love your spirit to bits & back.

love Sandra xx

24 September 2017

IT'S YOUR TIME

Copyright © 2017 Sandra Donald.

All rights reserved. No part of this book may be used or reproduced by any means, graphic, electronic, or mechanical, including photocopying, recording, taping or by any information storage retrieval system without the written permission of the author except in the case of brief quotations embodied in critical articles and reviews.

iUniverse books may be ordered through booksellers or by contacting:

iUniverse
1663 Liberty Drive
Bloomington, IN 47403
www.iuniverse.com
1-800-Authors (1-800-288-4677)

Because of the dynamic nature of the Internet, any web addresses or links contained in this book may have changed since publication and may no longer be valid. The views expressed in this work are solely those of the author and do not necessarily reflect the views of the publisher, and the publisher hereby disclaims any responsibility for them.

Any people depicted in stock imagery provided by Thinkstock are models, and such images are being used for illustrative purposes only.
Certain stock imagery © Thinkstock.

ISBN: 978-1-5320-1913-5 (sc)
ISBN: 978-1-5320-1912-8 (hc)
ISBN: 978-1-5320-1914-2 (e)

Library of Congress Control Number: 2017903721

Print information available on the last page.

iUniverse rev. date: 05/19/2017

Contents

Giving In with Dignity 1
The Light Has Gone Out! Or Has It? 2
You Left Too Soon 3
The Invisible Cloak 5
Thorn 7
Trust 8
Awaiting Repair in the Garage 11
Death to a Past 13
I Can't 15
I Matter 17
Not Quite Family 19
So Close but Miles Apart 20
Tears 21
Move On 22
Stumbling Blocks 23
Why Fear a Bully? 25
Minus Nine and White Droplets 27
The Child in Me 31
The Truthful Path 32
What Is Life? 33
Friends 34
Happiness 36
My Life Hope 39
Pandora's Box 40
The Masters of Trade 43
So It Will End 45
Walking Away 47
Aroma in the Air 49
Where Is My Romeo? 51
Four Simple Words 53
A Period in Time 55
Just Call Me PMT 56
It Feels Upside Down 57
Comeback Factor 59
Divine Grace 60
Glorious Applause 61

It's Your Time 63
Reaping 64
Voice 65
Fear 66
Tiredness 68
Stroke, What You Brought Me 69
All Lives Matter 70
Do We Know? 71
Fight Harder 73
London Burning 75
Prejudices 77
The World Is Outta Money 78
Blessings 79

Musical Words to Feed the Soul 81
Special Love 83
Your Smile 85
Friday Night 87
Let Me Stay 89
Tell Me 91
Stormy Weather 93
Friends 94
How Could You? 96
You Will Be There 98
Distant Love 100

The journey started in March 2009 when I became an international poet.

Traveling to Stage Tech Music College, London, I opened my monthly *Soroptimist International* magazine. The advert asked members to submit a poem based on the theme of hope, imaging women and children survivors of war in Afghanistan, Bosnia, Herzegovina, and Rwanda. My poem "My Life Hope" featured in the book *Voices in Verse* is raising money to help empower women and children to regain their lives. I read my poem at the book launch coinciding with International Literacy Day on September 8, 2009.

Life has a funny way of bringing us things that I call life's gifts—not necessarily things we would choose, and they usually come in threes. I believe they come to help us move on from stuck positions, sometimes a result of overthinking or good old procrastination instead of doing.

My first gift arrived in April 2007 when my creativity was gifted to me after my mother's death. A fountain of inspiration switched on, unbeknownst to me. It now sits alongside my faith, leading me on a new navigational journey, bringing words as inspirational poetry, musical compositions, and songs. Who can deny such friends!

It gave birth to D'Casio, singer-songwriter and international recording artist who creates music to feed the soul, as reflected in my soon-to-be-released album *How Could You?* As an artist, I have grown like a mustard seed and blossomed like a spring day. In the appendix, I will share some of my musical lyrics.

The next stage entrance arrived on Thursday, May 8, 2014, when I found myself at Chelsea and Westminster Hospital in London with a slow pulse rate and a doctor explaining he thought I could be having a heart attack. It started on Tuesday, May 6 with a sense of butterflies in my stomach, followed some weeks later by the traumatic loss of three-quarters of my hair. Next was the hoarseness in my voice, a visit to the ears, nose, and throat specialist, and an MRI scan in June to be told I had an underactive thyroid gland and a goiter.

The third appeared on October 30, 2015, with me waking up in the early hours of the morning to find my left arm and leg lifeless and unable to move. I was having a stroke. Once the dust settled, I knew *It's Your Time* would be written, forming part of my dreams and legacy.

As faith is my bedrock, it broke down resilience in grief to moving forward, offering up its beaming directional light. It taught me to accept that good things can come from painful experiences. Accompanied by a ride on a magical carpet with so much more to behold, I feel truly blessed.

Giving In with Dignity

Is it really nothing but a number?
That's shrouded in intrigue and mystery?
They say it's bad manners to ask,
And treason to ever my dear disclose.

Looking for lines and colors of gray,
It's been suggested that this maturity lark
Will give the game away when exposed
As a lie upon the grand entrance of
Mutton dressed as a lamb. Hee-hee.

Is it really all in a tonic jar that watches?
You sink deeper into its clutches whilst hoping
That you'll swim into the arms of extended youth.
The telltale signs are written on the wall,
Set out in a game called "bugger off and mind your own."

Tired and weary, you turn the corner and
See contentment supported by fulfillment,
With a glass full to overflowing where things
Can only get better with belief in self-acceptance
And embracing a joyfulness, yet more to come.

In continued age, you will not be dejected,
Invisible, or unwanted when you continue
To listen to faith's soft whisper directly,
Tapped into your soul to please accept
The many lessons passed this way and to come.

Push forward and revel in being a carefree spirit
On a path to greater heights where age and
Accumulated numbers are academic
When giving in with dignity!

November 16, 2011
Revised January 3, 2016

The Light Has Gone Out! Or Has It?

There was a light that burned with energy so fierce
That it lit up paths in its way for those known and unknown.
Its fiery flames of burnt orange and red often danced
In a joyous, contagious sway, igniting a warmth
In love with those most precious to it.

In the distance, a black cloud loomed, and the light
Watched it closely as slowly the darkness made
Its descent, smothering, till eventually it choked light,
Who, with its revitalized strength, fought back and
Regained its beauty and passion with a renewed vigor.
But quickly, without warning, the darkness engulfed light
Until the last flicker had been suppressed, and the light
Had no reserve to fight back.

The light has gone out, but has it when both its vibrancy and
Free spiritedness still seem to dance around in the air,
Spreading a continued playful affection of love,
With passion to those who see it vividly? They
Feel its essence and beauty burning brightly
In every direction they look.

So has the light gone out, or is it to remain
A treasured fixture that if you look hard enough
You might believe it was never extinguished?
Lights like these never diminish; they continue to grow.

May 2010

You Left Too Soon

Looking through the eyes of pain, I see hope calling me
With a smile that could mend a shattered heart.
As I reach her, I feel her positive energy as her breath
Reaches me, and with her gentle touch, she says,
"Hush, don't cry. You are still very special to me."

The light of life burns bright until life's certainties show up,
Taking away those special souls, erased with a rubber till they
Cease to exist in flesh, but their gift of life left in you remains
Burning fiercely, guiding you to your destiny as the first tear appears.

You left too soon, without a goodbye: no word, no cry or sigh.
And you were gone. I searched high, low in my mind and heart,
But I couldn't find you. I didn't see you disappear like a silent whisper.
Tell me when I will see you again 'cause you were gone too soon.
Will you tell me when I will see you again? 'Cause you were gone
too soon.

My mind is a swirl, clouded and misted in pain. Behind my eyes
Lies nothing but pain and a fading essence, taken away with
Its sharp, short intake and a voice that is barely audible.
I didn't see it coming. I was wrapped up in my life. I couldn't
Know it would feel this way until the first teardrop appeared.

You left too soon, without a goodbye: no word, no cry or sigh.
And you were gone. I searched high, low in my mind and heart,
But I couldn't find you. I didn't see you disappear like a silent whisper.
Tell me when I will see you again 'cause you were gone too soon.
Can't you tell me when I will see you again? 'Cause you were gone
too soon.

I'm lost in a maze, fighting my way back to the surface,
Gasping for air, determined to live and reclaim the legacy.
You left me the prize of life and all that it will give me.

You left too soon, without a goodbye: no word, no cry or sigh.
And you were gone. I searched high, low in my mind and heart,
But I couldn't find you. I didn't see you disappear like a silent whisper.
Tell me when I will see you again 'cause you were gone too soon.
Please tell me when I will see you again 'cause you were gone too soon.

September 19, 2013

The Invisible Cloak

My heart stopped dead
As I watched the life slowly leave.
It was like the last dredges of air in a balloon.
It collapsed and disappeared into a blackout room.
The intense sadness of tears fell like hail stones,
Hitting my face like a level five hurricane on the run.

A barely perceptible whisper
Moved into the atmosphere. "You will be okay.
Just believe it as your faith has taught you."
So why do I feel surrounded by mocking,
Taunting eyes muttering teasing messages?
"Did you really think life was a sunny beach in Cuba?
Well, not for you, not just now."

How did I not see deceit?
Conversing with liars, both holding hands,
Blocked from my vision whilst I busied with life,
Concealed like the Harry Potter invisible cloak.
They slipped by before revealing a one-eyed, withered snake
That plotted a destructive mixture of pain deeper than still waters.

But faith is a good ally
Who is always by my side in the front and back,
Alongside reliable hope, who is my champion.
So I say, do your worst. Watch me become stronger.
I can only thank you for the hurt and sorrow
Whilst you watch. Success will be the endgame.

December 4, 2011
Revised January 3, 2016

Thorn

A thorn slipped under my radar whilst intuition
Was prodding and poking me, but I turned the other way,
Saying I'm too busy to listen now. "Go away," I grunted.
It wore a disguised mask of a trusting smile whilst
Secretly laughing and reveling in plans to befriend me,
Dialing stress to smugly fit into that store called my life.

Digging deep into your skin, it twists. "Ouch," you squeal
When you see confusion and mayhem in the front-row
Seats, eating popcorn and enjoying a newfound power.
The game is tennis, exhausting to watch let alone play.
When you're not Serena Williams, it's not a game to match.

Your mind's first serve was tentatively played, trying to
Feel its way whilst unsure if it was a friendly or an out-and-out
Strategy to win the Wimbledon Cup. Please—what else is it!
The board showed a match point, and you know you must
Quickly decide if you must dig deep to defeat or compromise.
You could retreat and leave the thorn to play the game on its own!

Watching the thorn across the net, you start to see the shape
Of a vulture circling what it perceives to be a wounded animal,
Feeling Lady Luck has arrived, licking its lips, visualizing the carcass.
It will devour this feast fit for the appetite of the dark shadow
Of win and control, with an objective completely unknown.

Switching tactics, you send an urgent text to logic asking,
Who is the best trainer in developing undetected plans that, once
Served, will and must hit the target, thorn, with a force that
Will knock it reeling to the floor, powerless to recover? Match over.
Upon receipt, the fait accompli is served, and thorn looks
At the board and sees it's a 6–1, 6–2 win supported by logic,
Integrity, and pragmatic knowing its removal is a permanent one!

Intuition is a guide, an ally, a best friend for forever, whilst
Thorn is simply a pain in the —!

January 31, 2016

Trust

In acknowledging the past, I see quandary stuck
At the crossroad of change. She's prompting me,
Pushing that green light in life. It is all systems go.

I'm quiet in this moment as I try to listen to my heart.
I know I must safeguard her with all of my might.
She is bright, fun loving, and free-spirited in splendor,
But as I watch, why is she still crying?

I see tears like hail stones cascade like a waterfall
Of pain mixed with sorrow, and she's shouting,
"I'm bruised and oh so shattered." It's back to the
Fetus position, the protection of life.

See, the alarm siren was activated, her breathing,
The pattern so short it felt panicked, stricken.
Will its small vessels tied up in me just close?
She is searching in darkness and is looking for

Trust, who once in abundance is now burnt to a dust.
She notices Love, and its soul is extinguished,
Withered, exhausted, and in a coma, all laid out, no fight.
For nights, days, and the years, it's remained in this state.

It screamed, and it pleaded in tears of unthinkable cries.
They reverberated like a ball bouncing on cold walls.
Exhausted one day, it lay still on an altar and watched
It sacrificed like a lamb. It was slaughtered at dawn.

Now Trust sits shaking and trembling in fear.
Trust's eyes are of emptiness, the avenue to the soul.
Now veiled in steel, enclosed in a protective vault,
Both code and key patterns are still unknown.

You had it, gave it away for a reason discussed
With you and self that was hidden from view,
In a mirrored reflection, back dating into a past.
It's here and now, pleading; resuscitate it back into our life.

What can you offer in terms and conditions?
Enforceable collateral for its restoration or that
Continued tender embrace. The picture you see is
Caution. Is its safeguard a trained army positioned?

At the stair to Trust, with Heart encased in ivory tower,
It silently watches this gift and shouts, "Entry denied."
She longs for that feeling that used to lift her world.
Yet now unsure of its existence, Hope steps into

The framework with the board of directors.
"Scared, Anxious, Pain, and all associated chums."
The agenda to sign or not on the dotted line will release
Trust and its heart, possibly into uncertain fated arms.

The jury is out for this life-changing decision,
Yet if Trust could reach out and regrab what once was
Unwavering belief, the justice system of the
Universe and with all that he knows, then

As the custodian of the leap of faith, Trust knows
He will never let her go, so she tumbles or falls.
But with denial in place, what will Trust do?
The jury has left ...

March 24, 2015

Awaiting Repair in the Garage

Someone I trusted stepped on my heart, and
As they did, I sat and watched the life in it
Expel like a gentle mist leaving, heart gasping.
So resuscitation was given, and although
Emotions fought a brave fight, nothing more
Could be done to revive it into any state of being.
Lifeless and limping, it was cajoled with loving care,
Willing it not to give up but to come back and fight
And to leave trepidation behind in the corner, but
Sadly its life evaporated with the heir to the throne,
Despair in chief position, the Alice in Wonder cat.

The air became thick with a primeval, wrenching cry
For help that rivaled labor pains, except without
The euphoria of giving birth, of holding the baby
In your arms. You felt cheated all in one even whilst.
Although the labor process had supportive calls to take
Slow, deep, and controlled breaths and shouts of
"You'll be fine, not long to go," now you're told
Maybe six months, a year, or better still, call it
"An undefined lead time" with suicide and revenge.

Sitting ringside, rubbing their hands whilst placing bets,
They started to party! You see, as that teenager,
Weren't you told there would be romantic comedies?
With always a happy ending, but did the script
Get changed for a concrete block being dropped
From the greatest height onto an unsuspecting heart?
"Love and until death do us part" strangely were
Substituted for "a demon of intense pain, humiliation,
And its lifelong associated friend, heartbreak."
It seems a thief robbed you of the sunny beach script

With beautiful white sand, the sun, turquoise blue sea,
Plus a cocktail or two. Please note, the party's still going on!
Immediately the heart police were called to investigate.
At the crime scene, their first observation noted showing
Clear evidence of the sheep in wolf's clothing, with
Tracks showing a quick getaway by car, a plane,
Plus speedboat and reports to having been seen
Sipping Pimm's cocktails in a bar in a faraway land,
With maybe a new heart who seemed to be, yes,

Infatuated or possibly in love mode. How could this be?
The heart police advise it's a good source but to be confirmed!
They also wanted to know, how did it happen with such training?
There was total silence, and they asked, was trust in the lead?
Were boundaries of defenses and control checks removed indefinitely?
"And, yeah, was love allowed in the room?" they asked, shaking their heads!
"Shame," they said. "We see this all the time, so if you venture into it again,
Be more cautious, but until then, simply put a sign in your eyes
(The gateway to heart), stating the following, and you should be okay, love."

Heart plus its associated friends are in the garage awaiting repair.
At the moment, diagnosis and solution yet to be determined.
Currently its estimated time of return to the road is …?
But please watch this space and follow updates on Twitter!

January 29, 2011

Death to a Past

I see an uncomfortable past floating into the distance,
Carrying in its lap a broken and bruised heart, tears,
And a truckload of fears, pushing along so much pain.
It represented that of the middle eye of the storm,
But with a smirk on its face of "job well done," feeling
So self-assured you didn't notice the head ripped off.
It had turned and started to rise above the ropes, but
You remained captivated by the eyes of a gentle soul
That was a like a soft egg sprinkled with gentle,
Loving, warm, captivating eyes of melting brown sugar.
You failed to notice, hidden deep within a determined
Force, fighting for its life in a true gladiator assurance.
Its energy not to be reckoned with, you brushed it aside
With arrogance tightly in hand. *Again* you didn't notice
A quiet closing of the door and the snip bringing new life,
The undeniable umbilical cord from the giver of new existence.

See, it had given you years of survival taken for granted.
Then the consensus voted that now it was your time to die.
There was no proper burial, a headstone, a sign of love,
Words of endearment, or any grieving at the graveside.
Only a lone silhouette of a calm elegance that turned,
Walked away with no tears or wet tissue in hand for this death.
Instead, a joyous beating heart for the demise of an
Evil, sophisticated, unwanted presence that had rooted
Unknown, lurking in the shadows of mind, not as a friend
But in truth a powerful enemy filling up the well of life.
With so much unnecessary foolishness like a thief,
You stole so many years, but now may you rest in peace "not."
Please be sure you will never cross this door into this life again.
With victory on board and the fight resolved, things quietly
Started taking shape. Deep within, an allegiance had already
Formed with a past offering memories of smiles, joy, love, and
So much more, should one want to explore its almost happy ever after.

No longer is there a need to challenge you to pistols at dawn
When we have upbeat and happy on board, and let's face it:
You where always dispensable and in fact didn't like to say, but,
Well, your place is already filled. How do you like that!
Heart, body, mind, and soul have already embraced anew,
Living harmoniously with here and now and the wonders
It has to share from within its very own twenty-four-hour
convenience store.
So your game and trickery of mind hasn't worked when
You ultimately only served to strengthen my friend resolve.
It's time to say thank you whilst not wishing you well,
Just a very enormous, happy death to an unwanted past.

March 10, 2015

I Can't

How can I feel so much anger
Tinged with so many mixed emotions?
Why can't or don't I feel love
And compassion for you,
Like it's written I should do?
Deep within the darkness of Pandora,
The cycle needs free of this toxic brew,
Of destruction mixed with menacing kindness.

I don't want this, and I don't need it, but
It's taken up residence within me, and
It makes me want to hide in shame.

I can't love you like you want.
I see it like a shadow in the moon, bright in your eyes.
They are filled with memories wrapped
In a child long gone from your view somehow,
Yet in your final moments, we must and will resolve.

It feels like a Jekyll and Hyde plot
Unfolding, featuring a footballer sitting
On the lines, waiting for the systems to go.
A place were your presence is treasured,
When you don't know how this all fits.

Ignited like a spark, a stick of dynamite
Slowly burning to its end of this poison
Arrow that it will target on line.
You … we need to stop this now.
It's simply blowing up my mind.

I don't want this, and I don't need it, but
It's taken up residence within me, and
It makes me want to hide in shame.

I can't love you like you want.
I see it like a shadow in the moon, bright in your eyes.
They are filled with memories wrapped
In a child long gone from your view somehow,
Yet in your final moments, we must and will resolve.

In this time, we should be closer so our
Nights end in mornings of joy to the sound
Of sorrow playing heavenly harps and
Our souls wrapped in silky, laced gold.

I can't love you like you want.
I see it like a shadow in the moon, bright in your eyes.
They are filled with memories wrapped
In a child long gone from your view somehow,
Yet in your final moments, we must and will resolve.

July 15, 2015

I Matter

Why has this dark cloud come to visit?
What does it want but to eat away at my soul,
Baring a me it's not entitled to know?
In a state of bliss, I took my eye off the gate.
Then a chameleon disguised as a trusted friend,
It let itself in, and I watched as it sat down.
Close beside me, it talked in a whisper
So softly, engaging in codes of negative thoughts.
It silently nibbled at a weakness in short,
But I know and you knew you had to go.
You were living on borrowed time in short!

Like a leech attached to an intravenous drip,
You slowly fed off the blood of my soul
Until I resisted and fought back, till slowly
I began to blossom, nourished in strength.
You see, I had God on my side, and you knew
That you'd never survive a fate such as that.
It was time for the last supper of the
Silent destroyer known as depression.
My mind isn't for sale, and neither dreams
Nor my, me, and desires, which I took from your view.

See, I restored and downloaded them in supportive
iCloud with a password called unknown in kind.
Brazen and bold in all the years that you waited,
You thought you'd just walked in unnoticed, and
Like that dripping tap, you started the decay,
Knowing there would be no pop of a champagne cap,
No celebration, especially when your type
Isn't welcome in this home or my inner palace alone.
So don't leave your business card when it's destined
For the shredder, like data erased. So are those
Tiny footprints once etched in my mind.

I see them, the shackles broken in tatters, and
Guess why? Because I matter. You tried and
You failed to unbalance a state of being,
Not to mention this vibrant mind of mine.
I reached out and grabbed "I will and can do."
The game was over, and you're so truly busted.
That veil of uncertain sorrow no longer dances
In view of your glare. It has been lifted, elated in
A splendor of joyful happiness till it's
Running totally wild. Maybe, yes, maybe.
Now you've got it. I matter.

March 23, 2015

Not Quite Family

Flying above clouds,
Looking into the warmth of shared love and laughter,
A playful, fun place in each other,
An unspoken bond stronger than a hurricane.
I watch the dynamics of family life unknown to me
Unfold before my eyes.

A pain of discomfort
Mixed with a loneliness as if lost in a desert,
Searching for a remote to interact.
It feels like a visitor on a day pass in a maze.
I've become visible yet invisible in my disguise.
I step into the arena.

A hidden family life,
Its troubles mixed with secrets, not like the movies.
I flick the channels, watching a chameleon in full glow.
In this game, it's to know your status and that place.
Do you get or even know the rules?
Are you quite or could be?

But surely the strength within you, as powerful as it is,
Can hold its position, confident of having the ability
To exist without the support of such a bond.

I'm not quite family, but
I wanna understand and wrap my arms in its security.
I'm not quite family, but
I long to inhale its aroma of strength.
I'm not quite family, but
In the comfort of my world, I've learnt to survive.

So I can fly high above the clouds of life, not alone.

December 2, 2012
Revised June 8, 2016

So Close but Miles Apart

As children, we laughed with one voice,
Finished each other's jokes and sentences,
Unable to control those enormous belly laughs,
Joined in blood, inseparable in love.

Protective was our main goal,
Mutual love and respect entwined.
Worlds that emerged saw a unity of strength.
So when did it unwind, unravel at source?

Did a soft wind blow into one's mind,
Taking with it rays that shone in your heart?
Now blown out like that candle in the wind,
It's thrown us so many miles apart.

Tears may fall for what once was.
It can't erase a bond made by the gods.
Choices made unknown seemed sealed in fate.
Watching and loving, so close but miles apart.

September 2, 2016

Tears

He sees the full picture hidden from view,
Yet it doesn't stop the tears cascading anew.
The picture is blurred in my visionary eyes.
Things I can't take back are turning into something new.
Rewriting the script in this mind's eye must stop.
The sadness will pass, fading into the universe.
Trickling water from these eyes is kind in sorts.
Listen silently for the teachings in hidden words.
The wisdom will empower me in lessons unlearned.
Whilst I do this, give me the strength to accept
Tears sent from heaven are gifted and blessed.

September 3, 2016

Move On

Failure doesn't exist. It's a springboard.
It's a helpful teacher with a license to show you
A different, brighter pathway to exploring the greatness within you.

So let's take each lesson, learn, accept, and move on.

March 8, 2016

Stumbling Blocks

Once successful but not anymore.

Your job specification from a darker side
Was to sow destructive seeds into a child's mind and soul.
So you created an evil monster embedded in a mustard seed
That grew affirmations creating lies of total unworthiness,
Such that the small child felt it deserved and was nothing.
But deep within, a voice whispered, "Put on those boxing gloves
And don't you totally believe. See, together we will fight back."

You smiled in the face of the defenseless child
Whilst you firmly attached yourself to its back. And
During the many years, the message grew in confidence
Into a billion-dollar conglomerate empire, so powerful within.
Then Armageddon arrived. The battle commenced, taking no prisoners,
Offering no mercy in the extinction of this sinister, evil monster,
When swiftly without discussion it removed you from the child's back.

In complacency, a blinding light caught you off guard,
Engulfing you in a tunnel of flames so fierce it took
But a millisecond—and *puff,* you were nonexistent.
In its hands, the blinding light carried a profound prophecy,
Part of which contained joy in a creative self, unconditional love
Surrounded by angels that saw the child being lifted
High into the realms of heaven. It was game over, no reinvention.

Now a supportive, trusting monster surrounded the child,
Who vowed to empower, love, support, and provide an abundance
Of opportunities, it knowing the child would run into its arms.
Hosting its wildest dreams and basking in this ordained glory,
It would fulfill more than what was written on its day of birth,
Because open in front of it was a clear path no longer held back
Or wrapped up in stumbling blocks seethed in the past.

March 5, 2016

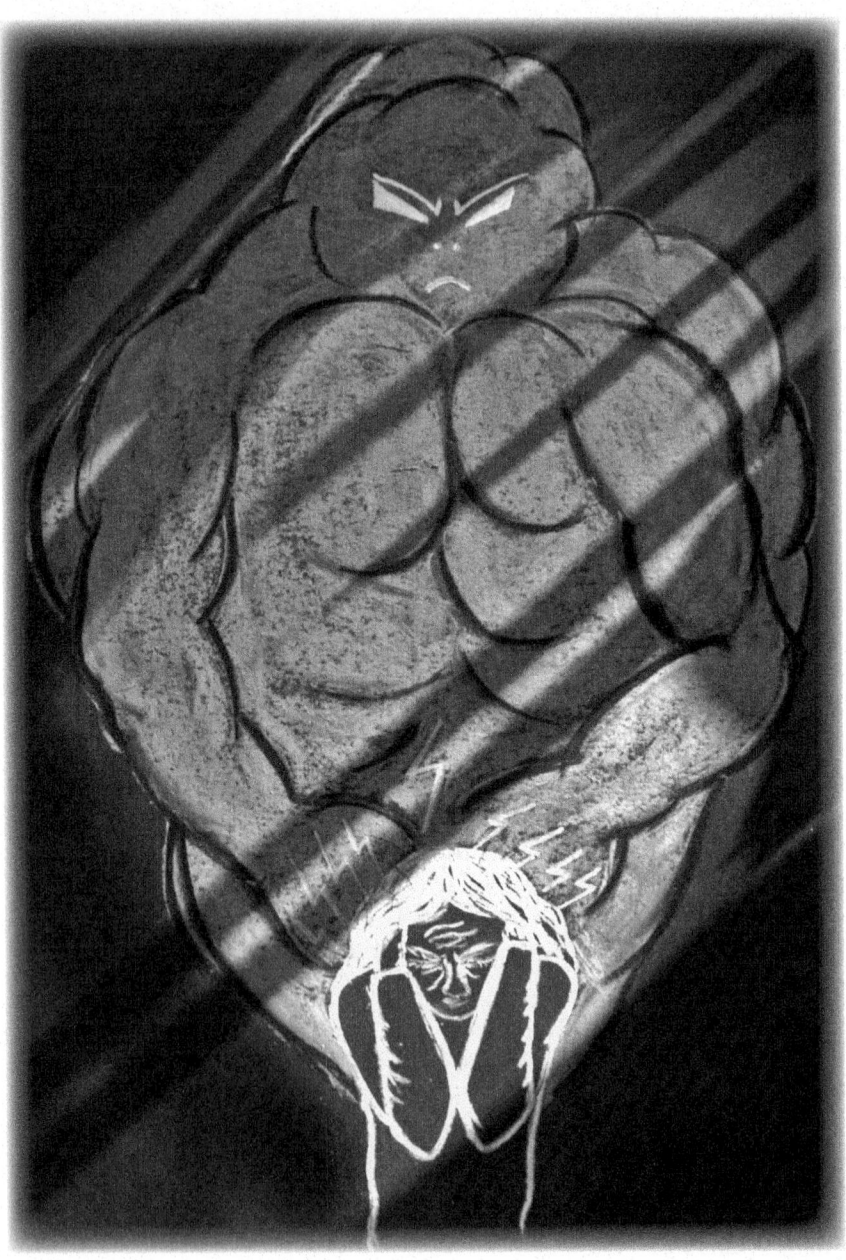

Why Fear a Bully?

Fear—how does it manifest itself and why?
Or is it really a bully and spineless coward!
In the wilds of the jungle, vulnerability is seen
As the next meal. The pouncing and devouring
Is to inflict pain that accommodates hunger
Of a continual survival. See, there's no Tesco
Or drive-through McDonald's to stock up.

In it, the victim hunted by the bully
Spins a game called "is it all in your mind," allowing
Paranoia in the da house to capitalize on your
Insecurities, now registered and called anxiety!
Watching stomach jump around with a sudden rapid
Distain for all food, even chocolate. Are you sick?

Was it fear of not being right and looking so different?
Not in right fashion and style or fear of getting
It so badly wrong that if the floor opened up and
Swallowed you, it would still be too painful to bear!
Whilst paranoia seeps through your veins, you
Give bully and its sidekick, coward, more opportunities
To inflict emotional and maybe physical pain! This must stop!

The warrior within screams, "Stand up to these idiot
Intimidator(s), tyrant(s) and let them see the color of
True inner strength in all it's shining glory before
Deciding to deal with fear, coward, copilot bully.
As the book says, "Feel the fear and do it anyway."
There is much truth in this statement if you take it
By the hand, turning bullies' pain into driven success.

But whilst you are caught in this moment of darkness,
In a still moment, find a quiet space in your mind.
Ask guidance and wisdom to show you the path,
To make the return journey back to sunshine and
Your friend positive, confidently sitting, patiently
Awaiting your return from a short break away.

Like Alexandra the Great, be ruthless, bold,
Unrelentingly challenging, succeeding
In your endeavors where others have failed.
With this aura surrounding you,
Watch fear, coward, and pitiful bully
Run for cover with their tails between their legs
Whilst you laugh at how pathetic they really are!

July 23, 2012
Revised July 27, 2016

Minus Nine and White Droplets

I hear there's something called
The minus-nine temperature. It's
Carrying multiplying white droplets
Called snow, who's whipping up a
Party called storm. Prepare London town!

Well, bring it on! The defenses are ready
And lined up to commence the battle.
Let's see exactly what is needed.

Hand cream:
Must be of the highest quality,
As dry hands on ladies don't work.

Gloves:
Thermal, thick, and chunky.
There will be an inspection
Of tog to ensure fingers
Can operate under the
Projected extreme conditions.

Lipstick of all shades welcome.
A line-up inspection to test the
Length of time before reapplication
Is required will be carried out before
Being given the okay to present
Yourself in a bag or hand for duty.

Snow boots:
No visible heel permitted, but
You must wait on the sideline and
Report for duty, which will only be
Under severe circumstances and
Where heels have malfunctioned,
E.g., broken off and busted.
You will not be called
To defend this extreme front line!

Coat:
Must have adjustable collar to cover
Where necessary ears/mouth and
With no means of allowing wind/air/snow
In will only be accepted for this mission.
No variation to this rule is ever permitted.

Hat(s):
Must be able to cover ears and
If necessary work in pairs doubled up.

Scarf:
Must be of a length to enable users to
Wrap around neck/face whilst permitting
Eyes visibility to detect the intruder and
Plot an effective escape route in seconds.

Thermal vest:
Mostly unattractive but is a very good,
Friendly supporter against the possible
Invaders of minus nine and white droplets.
When you need to dig in deep, apply two;
This will ensure maximum heat and a smile!

Tights/socks:
Must be able to provide maximum warmth
For those pretty toes and shapely legs' circulation,
Ensuring they can function and move with
Speed and accuracy against the looming enemy.

General clothes:
Take all things in wardrobe out and put them on,
And if you're unable to move, the following
Test should be undertaken.
- ❖ Stand still and swivel the top half of your body,
- ❖ Moving it from left to right, and if nothing happens,
- ❖ You may want to de-robe by a layer or two!

Failing any of the above, you may want to stay
In with fire, soup and bread, blanket, chocolate biscuits,
And watch from a distance the havoc that
Minus nine and white droplets cause in
Shutting down London city for days rolling by.

Don't take this the wrong way, but, winter,
I will always be so happy when you go away!

February 9, 2012

The Child in Me

I love that bold, mischievous energy in me
That encourages me to continue to be fearless,
Honest, and free-spirited, even in times
When I trip, falling, grazing my knees.
Or sometimes, frustrated, I shed a tear.

The innocence gives me the drive
To jump up and run off again, charging
At great speed toward my destiny,
Full of optimism, not caring how or why,
As if what happened was serious fun.
"Yeah, loving this!" it screams.

That look of wild abandonment
With a glint in its eye that says,
"I dare you to try to catch me."
One blink and you've missed it.

"Boom, I'm outta here," says the child in me!

June 6, 2016

The Truthful Path

Out of adversity comes greatness,
An awakening spurred on by focused ambition
Where you are driven by the desire to be the best.
Achieve, be successful, and be recognized by peers
As the talented person you were born to be!

This could be a mother, the most important of all roles,
Who uses her intuitive skills to nurture and guide
A loyal and trusting friend or partner. The choice is yours!
We have hope, a strong and unwavering friend,
Determination, and unconditional love.

As supporters, they breathe strength in us
Till we are sturdier than kryptonite.
They allow us to be fearless in the faces of lions.
Facing impenetrable walls, still holding the reins
In our hands, we claim what is rightfully ours.

No prisoners taken, no stone left unturned.
The desire as strong as air we breathe
Itself. It's your faith, the belief in that you can
Carrying you to the finishing line. You take
Your place among the stars, kings, and queens!

Once you recognize your destiny,
Own it and never doubt that natural ability
Given to you at birth, allied to your rightful heritage.
It's your only real path, the truthful path.

July 6, 2012

What Is Life?

Life is too short.
Heard it so many times.
But when the dream finds you,
Allow it to take you to the top
Of its mountain to shine in its success.

Open that parachute,
Pull the chord, jump.
Don't look back or procrastinate.
Enjoy the journey, bumps and all.
Believe that what awaits will blow
All expectations in your mind.

May 6, 2016

Friends

I thought it was us.
I thought it was we.
Yet somewhere along the road
I misread some of the traffic signals
And came off the road into a tree.

How easy was it to trust,
Giving one's self because of love
Or something perceived as that!
Can this word that lurks in doorways
Remain unregulated or quantified?

Do you see the casualties
Of the concept of love
Strewn across the globe?
Do you see them clutching remnants
Of nothing in particular, just a stare?

Staggering into the doctor's,
Demanding the cure, a prescription,
Being told no pill cure has been found!
Falling into heaps of despair and feelings
Escalating to fever-pitch screaming,
In a queue with a global waiting list
Of a trillion to one, no after-care support!

In the bright sunlight,
The light hits their skin.
It hurts. With shame, they shrivel
Into nonexistence, wanting someone.
Stop the memories, please. Ease the pain.
You see, it's crying time again!

It's comfort time.
Chocolate, drink, sex,
Isolation, solitude, fate, and options.
From the side benches, they wail, "Why me?
Did I do something wrong in an earlier life?"

Luck is here.
Follow the rainbow
Into the arms of friends,
Listening, comforting, with magical hugs,
With genuine understanding, gestures, and nods,
Coaxing, teasing, and over time repositioning.
It reignites hope back into your existence.

Gear stick in reverse, you back out of the tree,
Hazard lights flashing, deflated confidence on board.
Steering onto the road with visibly stitched wounds,
You slowly edge back out onto life's unknown road.

Glancing into the mirror,
You see friends
Driving closely behind.
Yes, it's time for a very wide smile!

February 27, 2011
January 3, 2016

Happiness

Maybe it was never released
Into the atmosphere because,
Like a child, it requires
Continued personal development,
Drops of love and nurturing
So it can become a black beauty
Bounding across the hills, seen
Racing through valleys,
Outshining the greatest of stars.

Maybe it's sitting patiently waiting
For us to call upon it to make
Sure its presence is radiating brighter
Than the sun in lighting up the world.
See, it has an unchallenged free spirit.
Traveling with an unknown compass
To every corner of the globe, it moves
Undetected, crossing all border zones.

No need for visas or letters of introduction.
Its entry is that of an indefinite stay.
It's never asked, "How will you finance yourself
When you are staying in this country?"
If embraced before the onset of wars,
Then peace would take the place
Of the ugliness that is visibly laid bare,
Exposing unnecessary pain and suffering
Inflicted on the weakest of mankind.

The flip side to this is mix it with love.
It has the potential to propel special moments
Beyond the imaginable realms of a seat on cloud nine!
I wonder, can I hold you in my hand?
If I could, what would it look like?
What would be your smell? How would it feel?
Would there be timbre in its voice if it has one,
Or does it softly talk to you in still moments,
Trying to shift moods into that brighter zone?

It really is invisible to the naked eye,
With energy that surrounds us in
A 365-degree rotating glare.
If we could only be brave enough
To daily inhale its magical aroma,
Our lives in this world would benefit
From an existence of an unspoken harmony.

If only we called on happiness more often!

February 7, 2016

My Life Hope

Hope is a drug and has the strong hold on my heart.
It's with me first thing in the morning
And as I lay my head to rest at night.
Like coffee, it's that adrenalin rush
When everything around me seems to be falling apart!
Reaching out through the darkness in
Despair, I find hope unshaken but not stirred, shining so bright!

Hope moves within me with every intake of breath.
Its inspiration brings a knowing that better things are to come,
And with its open hand it gives me the courage to close
The door on all negative thoughts as I glance over my shoulder.
I see hope waiting, and I calmly walk toward its burning light of hope.

Hope provides me with the positive mind-set
To afford continued good health.
It gives me the strength to keep showing love,
Allowing myself to be loved and to support and
To care for those I love the most.
It fills me with a strength and boldness,
Which drives me to continue on life's paths
With a focused determination but always with my friend hope.

So let's have three cheers for hope.

February 2009

Pandora's Box

Apply and leave for fifteen minutes.
Sit back and ponder your expectation,
Visualizing it from a central position.
Give the mind space and time
To think, analyze, drift, and ignore
As it dances with truth, wisdom, and honesty.

The true reflection is in the mirror.
Is it the same as before but wiser?
Do you hear the tiny voice?
Will you listen to its advice?
With pouted lips posed to speak,
You see the box, the holder of all.

A smile curves on your lips.
Out comes a hi, and eyes go warmer.
In the distance is a tidal wave
Of wild emotions perched in the middle.
He offers you a welcoming hand.
Do you choose to take it or walk away?

Suggested a journey to dark turmoil,
Slowly and provocatively turning.
Your shoulder brushes him aside,
Stepping into sunshine and control.

Pandora offers lessons learned and to come.
Her box is filled of life that can be warm,
Enchanting, captivating like fire, or
Freezing cold as an iceberg in June
Whilst staring you straight in your eyes!

October 4, 2013

The Masters of Trade

Could do better, the phrase that conjures up a must-try-harder person
Who is often never perceived to be good or even average?
What's the remedy, recipe for such a beast?
Who has the methodology to impart the knowledge and support?
Yet can in seconds move you to shame from zero to ten?

Does it lie within, their built-in confidence mechanism?
Or does it require old-fashioned application, dedication, and
Determination to become the best and move them to their
Rightful place along the side of the many stars?

Talent, willpower, and hard work are all key players
In helping "could do better" jump the many hurdles to success.
But which one of them is the weakest link?
They must root out the conspirator so as to avoid the shout,
"Goodbye. You are the weakest link."

The light is focused and rested, still on "unable to pull its weight,"
Who is seen fleeing the vicinity. The pressure is on for "could do better,"
Whose scrutiny is seen by numerous eyes, sitting with "thoughts and opinions."
The matter will be assessed at the job appraisal interview, no stone
Unturned. It will tease out of an agenda steeped in secure, tested goals.

Talk is gentle, tinged with severe remonstrating of letting down.
Failure has now been evoked with instructions for you to leave this job,
Whose vocal prowess triggered to utter the words, "Leave. You're fired."
"Could do better" knows it must seek out masters of the trade.

They have been on this road and understand how to make it
Through this pain barrier. Dig deep. In guidance, you must apply
The same tactics so as to succeed were others have failed
Whilst, within a breath away from the masters, "could do better"

Watches like a hawk, attaching its mind and all fibers on fire.
Presses the button for the transfusion of knowledge to slowly seep in,
Knowing it will soon take its places alongside "good and excellent."
Beaming with renewed confidence, "could do better" is seen.

Sitting alongside "excellent and honors" is "could do better."
Ecstatic but not pushy, parent whooping, shouting,
Clapping out of control, pointing. "That's my child!"
The masters of trade just bring it on!

March 1, 2011

So It Will End

We have to stop this battle and agree when it will end.

It's killing love that once shone bright
Like a beacon radiating in glorious light.
Love is confused, casted under a dark cloud.
It feels battered, lost at sea whilst crashing against the waves,
Drifting like wood, with no port or clear direction in sight.

The journey, it started years ago, inclusive of promise
And friend vigor. They both took seats on a majestic
Banqueting table of ladies, lords, kings, and queens.
But like the *Titanic* did it collide into a glacier and
With time slowly sink, becoming a shipwreck,
Embedded deep within the ocean, now its home.

The thing is the incision inflicted by the glacier
Is still bleeding and seeping unnecessary blood
That has to be stemmed, so it injects much-needed
Revitalization into renewing the lives drifting at sea,
Exposed to a wilderness, becoming reproductive coral,
Feeding off a line bait of ego, a self-destructive element.

What fools were we to not simply just back down!
Confusion muscled in teasing love and happiness
That both shrieked out, "Break free from this, idiotic fool,
Or face an unwanted fate spiraling out of control."
With sense and sensibility closing in on the craziness,
They waved their hands with despair, and sitting close
On all heels, they all screamed with unimaginable decibels,
"You must deny a feast to the circling birds of prey!"

The clash of the Titans was a war of the gods, but
Who needs to rule when the universe has an
Abundance wrapped up in love, waiting for you?
It was decreed it was time to ditch the maybe
Cause(s) of egos, stubbornness, and a certain
Depressant personality high, and let's dare
To be courageous and fight back to win.

Or are we to become mutinous in our dealings
That we shall grab the reins of our life in both our hands
And turn the ship around back into our command?
In triumph together, we will chart a trip to break out
Of this prison, and with total strength, we will cut free
The chains linked to what was a shipwreck and weighty anchor.

We will slowly, shaken not stirred, be guided safely
To the likes of Kilimanjaro's mountaintop, and with
Reinforced life skills we will split free of the entwined coral
Who now, with pained and wet eyes, helplessly watches us
In our progress push forward in strength and with victory.
In joint hands, all served up within our might.

We will turn with grace, and with a royal wave
God will bless our ship setting sail into a new world
Of a positive beginning, with all confidence on our side, and

So it will end.

March 31, 2015

Walking Away

It's time to use this pain of apparent death
To bring me closer to what my soul
Came back here to achieve.
From the goodness of the plant of life
I will extract the positives, like
The saltwater from the sea, and
Use its natural remedies to heal
This wound. Feeling the blessings
Of God lifting me up above the skies,
Parasailing me directly into the heavens.

The past is what we had. It was a place
Where my corner was yours,
A time when I gave to ensure your
Happiness and allowed it to be taken.
You knew the vulnerabilities and
Effects of actions that would cut
Open wounds, unable to heal, like
That experienced by a parent of a lost child.

Peeled back to the skin like an orange
Sliced with a sharp knife, you watched
The sweetness of the juice drain out of it
With a macabre sense of satisfaction.
As the pain ran down and stuck to heart,
It squirmed for years like a fly
Caught in a spider's web, slowly suffocating,
And with its weak pulse, it should not have survived.

The stealer of a birthright but not of the spirit
Living within it handed over a strategy
That lifted weary, feeble eyes and guided it
With unknown hands to turn the survival key,
To lock shut this door for evermore.
You see, it's been open too long, waiting
For a return when every fiber knew
This would not and could not be undone.

Done with trying to figure out if you do
Or don't love me any more or whether
Blood is actually thicker than water.
With a proud head held high 'cause
I'm so tired of being tired, of trying.
The angels know the full story, and they

See the hidden tears wrapped up
In this sense of one-sided love.
I wish you well, and maybe in
Another life it's a better ending.
For now, I will love you always.
You are my blood, but it's time
To be walking away.

April 27, 2015

Aroma in the Air

If love is an aroma that fills the air,
Then we need it as we do oxygen.
Deny it entry into your life, and
You will starve as if stranded
In the Sahara Desert sand dunes.

Watch it when it takes center stage
Light up with a presence brighter
Than the greatest performers of all time.
Nothing can dim love's power.
Its ability increases one's inner strength to
Move mountains, projecting an outer beauty
That if bottled would be the front cover of *Vogue*.

Its heartfelt pain and loss can make it wither
If not challenged to change into positives.
Uplifting it inspires a greatness to behold.
Feel its energy like that of waves in an ocean
As it moves secretly through you and in you,
Ever consuming all that you are in body and spirit.

Its secrets delight, simultaneously touching places
That can bring on tears of joy, sorrow, and indifference.
If I or we are ever powerful through technology
Of Facebook, Twitter, iPhone, science, and the moon,
Why not strong or intelligent enough that we can
Put out the need for love of self, family, or friends?

April 27, 2011

Where Is My Romeo?

As mist disappears into nothing,
So can love. If starved of water,
It will whither and die
Like an unwatered flower.
Its place, a state of complacency,
Lying undetected for years
Till it forms a steel-plated
Drawbridge with armed defense lines.
Impenetrable to cries of love, it
Looks to escape to the hills of happiness.

Reconciliation is banished
Into the bowels of the forest,
Seen with an overgrown beard,
Long, unmanicured nails,
Bulging, red, puffy eyes, and
A faraway, starved, glazed
Look in its eyes. It sees
Love, who sat at the fireplace,
Encased in a steel, armed bank vault
With an unknown security code.
Hyperventilating, it's gasping
For affection that's failed to appear.

Recall sometimes makes an escape,
Drifting back into the past where there
Is a lightness of the remembrance of love.
The painful ending often crushes it,
Leaving intense hurt inflicted, minus shame.
In the distance, there is a constant knock-on-wood
Effect where hope sits in his makeshift cave.
He is wise, always forgiving, positive, and
Holds a full cup of everything except injustice.
He prods, cajoles, whispers into your heart
Moving soul and slips under the radar of detection.

He sees a light of hope, but it's overshadowed
By fear of rejection, the exposure to be seen,
To want to retry. And sadder still, an unwillingness
In admitting any possible regret, or even greater
Still, a love that would not have died had it
Not been for the lack of food and water.

Oh, Romeo, where for art thou!
Unfortunately not here with me yet!

July 13, 2011

Four Simple Words

I said to my child, "Take responsibility for your actions.
And when you're wrong, stand up and own up so
Your character isn't tarnished and difficult to repair."
"Thank you, Mummy," said the child, "for your kind words."

"How many times do I have to say slow down,
Don't run, take your time, because when
You're older, time will varnish like unseen
Vapors in the air." *Bah humbug*,
Thought the child, but said,
"I'm sorry, Mummy. I appreciate your wisdom and time."

When you fell down with knees bruised
So sore you rushed at great speed into my
Arms, where I scooped you up, kissing you,
Your knees till they and you felt brand-new,
"All better?" I asked.
"Yes, Mummy. I'm sorry, Mummy, for causing
You so much concern, but thank you, Mummy,
For always being there to make things seem so right."

As years passed unseen, the wrong crowd took
The reins, bringing unforgotten rules of humanity.
Memories of unconditional love wrapped
In values instilled with such care and attention
To detail that one day would bring a smile.
See, in her role, she had packed a goody bag
To embrace the world full of basic skills
That in your Gulliver's travels trip
Around the globe, in the pursuit of happiness,
They would see kings marvel in awe
Of this kind spirit and gentle, beguiling soul.

Instead an allegiance was formed with
New allies like Arrogance, Not My Problem, and
Why Should I Care watching in full view, the head
Held in shame with words of "why" perched
On her lips. I said, "These be my crew I hang with now."
I spun round mocking, and even as Remorse
Begged me to embrace Apologize or even Regret,
I clung to Self-Centered Behavior and
Switched on my iPhone, laughed in their faces
Whilst saying, "Hey there. What's up. Yeah,
That's good. I'll see you in five."

Battle lines crossed, up stepped Be Humble.
Like fog, it crept up under the door, and with
Weeping eyes, it stated a case to release me
From the chains of Arrogance and its
Associated friends encased in loss of respect for self
And the ability to acknowledge basic courtesy
Till God said, "Sit down. Listen. Let's get you back
Right on this track." "I'm sorry and thank you," I said.
I know it's all about those four simple words.

July 24, 2012
Revised June 8, 2016

A Period in Time

Does it drop by when expected?
Is it a known, groomed inconvenience
That starts the mind jumping in and out of radar
Into a sometimes not so happy zone?

Cravings burst into action, outperforming
Tweeter hits, and sugar's a new soul mate.
Rage takes a backseat, yearning in splendor.

It's not about being sick,
Although maybe slightly wounded.
You show your teeth to all who dare
As they approach with extreme caution.
It's nearly over, and feeling relieved,

Another monthly period is over ...

October 4, 2013

Just Call Me PMT

It sometimes comes when expected.
Its inconvenience is always known.
On queue, mood starts to jump around like Trigger.
The *Evening Standard* front-page breaking headlines read as follows:
    "Chocolate consumption wins 9 BAFA awards
    whilst outperforming all divas."
    "Cake has become a true and lasting soul mate."
    "Rage runs riot simmering nicely on an even low heat whilst you
    ain't too proud to beg him to take a backseat and just chill."

"I'm not sick!" you shout. "I'm just an unpredictable hormone
Who's a slightly wounded lioness on twenty-four-hour parole."
In a roar, you flash razor-sharp teeth to all who dare,
Snarling, approach with extreme caution.
It's another monthly period. Beware!

February 21, 2016

It Feels Upside Down

The world has no boundaries.
I can see your written thoughts
Dipping in and out of a faceless existence,
Shared in friendship with thousands unknown.

This public domain, is it collective?
If it is, with what and with whom and why?
Is it interaction with souls that matter or even know?
Or a platform for acquiring impersonal friendship?

Membership is free with hidden costs,
A place to give up hidden treasures and more,
To set sail secret ideas that swirl toward a faceless crowd.
One click, and its nonretrievable, lost in cyber space.

Is it an arena to seek out validation?
Where self-worth is disguised as being sociable,
Where in this window's eye, you see war, unwarranted violence.
Sitting in solitary isolation on Mars, watching the twenty-first century,
You are seen shaking your head, simply perplexed.

You mumble in disbelief, "It feels upside down,
Confusingly wrong to release so much information
Into the guardless frontier of the universe," thinking
It's maybe time to switch it all off and just talk.

May 6, 2016

Comeback Factor

When that stormy weather is relentlessly beating
On your door, it's time to dig deep into the arms of faith.
If you look and listen, you'll see the comeback.
Its factor is holding out her hand that is leading you
To join forces with hope and determination,
Whilst focus is steering you into the arms of your dreams.

Let's big up the comeback triple factor!

December 2, 2015

Divine Grace

Leaving empty isn't a choice;
It's a must reality that's
Happening in minutes now.
Secure in your belief mechanism,
Embedded deep visions seem
Through blinking infrared eyes.

It serves you like an invisible
Fragrance destined to manifest
True greatness, unwilling to sit on the sidelines.
Can you see its exquisite brightness?
Dazzling sunglasses are needed to shield.
The outpouring of excitement watches it
Kick open the door, running careless

Yet controlled in decisions.
Feeling liberated, it's born free,
Energetic, yet awe inspiring.
Joyfully in love with its ultimate legacy,
It will empty what is meant to be,
Divine grace shining glorious in your hands.

June 18, 2016

Glorious Applause

With tears falling like energy in music,
Walking, searching for that golden door,
Why must my shoulders keep shaking
Till there's a waterfall representing my face?
I'm still breathing in belief encased in my strength.
It whispers to me in the distance, "Almost there."
With a breath in a soul, it's so close I inhale its secret essence.

Dizzy, lost in a maze of uncertainty,
Turning, shouting, no more faceless shutters.
Slamming, bang, tight intuition beckons and is calling.
She knows there's a raging fire of passion burning bright,
So out of control, waiting to explode. It must come to fruition.
Knees, clasped hands are sore, contained in a mind driven in hope.
The doors are open wide. Smile. It's your friend, glorious applause.

June 2, 2016

It's Your Time

I have sailed through seas treacherous and calm.

I'm now ready in time for you to steer me
In the direction to the north or south, leading to destiny
Whilst I bring this ship about to its final conclusion.
I will drop the anchor to regroup, assess, restock so
I can make those subtle changes and once again set sail.

When I was sitting on the ocean bed, I became
Invisible to the sharks sailing a millisecond from my heartbeat.
Instead I swam with the dolphins, marveling at the natural energy
That surrounded me like a protective cocoon till we became one.

I showed respect for this powerful power source
That can close its back door anytime with no warning,
Such that life's journey can end, and you surface no more.
I know I did. It gave me grace to swim onto greater shores.

Making my way to the top, did I meet the eye of the storm?
Was it mixed with confusion, uncertainty, or was I greeted
By my trusted allies in crime, determination and associate grit
That enabled me to sail at unregistered knots to that the finishing line?
I know I did every time!

Charting my course, I set out, my map of life before me.
In doing so, I looked at the current position and marveled
At the past achievements, crying, ever grateful and proud.
I even gave thanks to the tears and sleepless times
Collected on the way that had holistically nurtured me,
Bringing me this far.

Moving forward, I held my trusted pen.
It plotted my navigational journey that would
See me leap over mountains undone in history,
Onto dry land in record time, lifting me up high
Into the heavens and the golden trophy called
It's Your Time.

May 28, 2016

Reaping

A farmer sits alone in his cold and unwelcoming home, praying
his harvest this year will be plentiful.

He thinks back over the year and recalls the early mornings up
before the birds and asleep just before dawn.

He believes his call is to produce the best crops in the world
so he can be pleased with his achievement based on passion
and a true love to create all things good for the customer.

He knows that if he gets it right, it will bring him great
financial reward, but it won't stop him from getting his
hands dirty again for next year to repeat the same and even better.

He forgets the tears, backache, and sleep deprivation
when he sees his produce in the best of all shops, enjoyed
by all who will benefit from the nutritional value in his goods.

They will become strong, with alert minds, energetic bodies,
and as he holds his vegetables in his hand, and it turns to gold before
his eyes.

He knows they are reaping what he has sowed. And he thanks the Lord!

October 4, 2013

Voice

You are my:

Glory hallelujah, that Christmas in June;
Cartier fifty-carat diamond bling, plus much more;
Treasure trove wrapped in divine, heavenly bliss;
Army of angels singing harmonious praise;

Sexy, sassy, nasty, smooth chocolate;
Center stage star lifted up high;
Substance deep in my soul;
Very precious and rare gift.

TripAdvisor rated
"Five stars, plus, plus, plus, absolutely amazing."

Mine to cherish on our handheld special journey!

February 24, 2016

Fear

Nothing short of a criminal trying to shortchange you
Of your birthright, so beware to lock all invisible doors
With a beguiling smile and a charming manner
That melts butter and the coldest of hearts. Fear
Stretches out its warm and clammy, deformed hand.
You take it, and it grows like a weed in unlit,
Wet, dark zones where it seeks out the mind, body, and soul.

It burrows and digs deep along with its friend,
the dripping tap, until the smallest of holes
Is secured and it's in home dry. See, no pneumatic
Drill needed now, just a static patience in kind.
With its residency secure, it settles in on the sofa and,
Watching that fifty-two-inch plasma TV, sometimes heard
Singing out loud, dancing, drinking champagne, and
Feasting on the finest food in our minds, all at your expense.

Its even convinced our friend dreams that it's wasting
Its time and how on earth can you possible believe
You can achieve greatness? Aren't you just a silly Billy!
With confidence record high at 150 percent and growing,
Its relationship with vulnerability has become
Inseparable; they are the BFF in the entire world.
With such a conceited position, fear failed to cover all bases.
Unseen on the sidelines sat a stalwart, determined child
Whose dummy sat spitting in rage and dug in heels.

It quietly says, "You will not take away my BFF, dreams."
With gritted teeth, slanted eyes, the determined child
Looked up with tears falling from its eye and softly,
Saying within to Fear, "You have no place here because
You are not and cannot be a reality in this life.
I promise I will make you go away!"
With no warning, the determined child jumped
Up and down on fear with an innocent, unknowingly,
But with accidently on purpose approach, knowing.

Till fear turned blue and the determined child,
With one swipe, snatched back its dreams.
Fear's downfall was its inflexibility to exist within
A loving environment, which suffocated him until
He became a victim without warning of mutinous
BFFs who, without consultation, catapulted
The determined child to sit amongst the stars.

Now, with absolute resolve, the determined child sat
Opposite fear and, looking sweetly at a lifeless fear,
Smiled and said, "You must have known that what
Is already written in the tablets of stone cannot be changed."
So it's with pleasure that as we start a new year saying,
"Fear, here is your job notice. Leave. Go elsewhere to seek
Alternative employment. No vacancies for you here."

January 3, 2016

Tiredness

The cloak of darkness slowly sweeps over,
Undetectable but deadly. Carry such heavy legs,
With arms weighed down, slowly sinking.
Like the *Titanic,* you feel trapped in quicksand,
Reduced to movements of a programmed robot.

The hiss in mind has become a piercing buzz,
Sounding like a swarm of bees. It's a surreal and
Floating sensation as fatigue takes its stranglehold
Whilst tears wait eagerly by the sidelines, watching
Appetite and stomach flee the creeping tiredness,
Starting to make its presence, so ever unwelcome, known.

It stares you in the face with a defiant glare and challenges
Sense, sensibility, and reason that all fled life's arena
As you hold your head in your hands with questions of,
Why aren't I able to move with these aching shoulders?
They feel like the world's permanent resting home.
You cry out to help. No response, just a red flashing light
Of danger. No sound from within, just emptiness equals grim.

You seek comfort in tears, asking why in a scream.
How did it all become so totally out of control? Don't tell me
I should have stopped catching my breath. I tried, but it escaped,
And so I did just one more thing. It had to be done.
Logic asked, "Was or is it so important?
Risking pushing so close to the edge? You see, my dear,
There's no return in time, health, or monetary matters."

Future enters the ring, speaking to soul, screaming at
Piercing pitch, "The goal is to watch, listen for alarm bells."
These sirens rang in the Second World War. It's a bomb attack.
They called your name, saying are you silly. Avoid it because
Casualties are hospitalized with reckless, carefree, and stupid.

Tiredness is a friendly warning if only we'd listened to her.
Take her advice to stop and recharge the Duracell battery of life!

February 25, 2012

Stroke, What You Brought Me

Starlight so bright it dazzles.
Treasures so rare, transparent in full glare.
The revitalization of an energetic power within this soul.
Opportunities in abundance unique that they will dare.
Kindred spirit wrapped in stars of gold.
Everlasting glory in praising the Lord.

So thank you for dropping by with such a wonderful array of gifts.

March 1, 2016

All Lives Matter

I watch from my window. It all seems the same,
Similar fears and interests wrapped in desires.

There is a difference as reflective like the sun.
The ceiling is different, confined in a box.
It hosts categorized labels and what
Talking, cajoling, reaching out to those
Reclining in generational privileges,
Ahead in the life game. An audible silence
Is screaming "It's time for an even match.
Push," it says, "and you'll find the handle."
It's the volt hosting equality in abundance.

Do we need a wall divider wrapped up in hate?
Breaking it down reveals rows of irrational,
Fearful, nonsensible behavior that somewhere
Over the rainbow lay fairness and justice for all,
A garden place where all lives matter, striving
To build, in true greatness together, sheltered
Communities of harmony, a rainbow melting pot
Mixed up in their differences, working in synergy.

See, we don't need any more civil or global wars.
We need to develop a space in that all lives matter.

September 6, 2016

Do We Know?

Elected into time,
We trusted you with our world,
Handed you all faith
Wrapped in trust.

Money feeds violence.
Lost in pride,
Created into tears,
Destruction lies.

I see those pleading eyes so desperate in hope.
I watch heartbeats so lost. Where is there love?
Look at the silent children dazed in play.

Do we know best in the west?
Where millions of lives have been lost.
Do we know best in the west?
We've created cities without homes.
Do we know best in the west?
We've left countries and dead, empty souls.
Tell me what we know.

Restricted in reports,
Words played in minds.
Negative was its best, oh, what a mess.
A culture unknown, never trying to understand
Reality, checked its no game, but maybe we lost.

We gotta tear down walls and bring up a new generation.
We must stand up tall and bring in a resolution.

Do we know best in the west?
Where millions of lives have been lost.
Do we know best in the west?
We've created cities without homes.
Do we know best in the west?
We've left countries and dead, empty souls.
Tell me what we know.

August 24, 2016

Fight Harder

If we managed to live in peace,
To eradicate poverty,
Overcome terrorism,
Could we live in harmony?
What do you think?

Questions overwhelming for logic to bear.
See, she knows what is involved, the many factors, like
Talking with respect with an outstretched hand
Wrapped in dignity reduces blood pressure highs,
Whatever they must be, allowed into all arenas,
Bottom up and not just up maybe down.

Disharmony seems to fit nicely by getting
Fearful results, who is seen rubbing
Their hands, maybe in glee, laughing, seeing.
Again they are easy to entice into another
Fruitless game, moving their eyes and not
Seeing water is slowly ebbing away.

Alongside ozone layer wishing them
Farewell, adieu, and even so long.
Watch blame pointing at each other.
See what will it matter when thirst
Starts to claim all lives, irrespective
Of color, culture, wealth, or indifference.

We forgot to fight harder for environment and water!

July 23, 2016

London Burning

Like the Black Death, it engulfed the city of London,
Settling dust in the air. These rats carried the plague,
Swarming the city, pillaging and raping its goodness,
Causing destruction, sorrow, and robbing people
Of their lives and their peaceful existence.
They came like locusts to rob and loot, wearing hoods
Over their heads. The black balaclavas saw only
Glaring eyes instilling fear to approach.

London stood still in horror as clouds of darkness
Saw the air infiltrated with hatred for authority.
This, their birth country, they said had failed them,
Disowning them, doing many wrongs unrighted.
Yet in passing it had provided free health care,
Free education, housing and ceiling opportunities,
Even envied in other countries in the world.

The mob mentality carried wealthy opportunists
Schooled at the higher end, unthinkable to most.
People asked, how was this addressing their needs?
Were they fighting to address the cause?
Do they live in housing estates littered
With poverty, in fear, with limited prospects
Of breaking free the chains of any injustice?
It was good to hang out, returning to their lives.

For many, it was a stage voice to addressing
What they saw as a "them and us" vibe,
Marginalized in a dysfunctional environment.
Compensation attracted a shady gang life, so
Armed with cars filled to breaking capacity,
They drove into the night whilst London burnt.
Community leaders cried into their pillows,
"What will become of our children, nephews, and nieces?
Why did they do this, what did we do so wrong?"
Questioning, were they to blame for these unhappy souls?
Or maybe they felt a sense of entitlement was long
Overdue, and collection time was on this night!

Let's stop and think. Were some afraid to fight
To get that good education, work hard for years to
Achieve/aspire so they could hold their heads
Up high, blazing a trail in communities filled
With low esteem, needing a solid role model?
Parents raised voices against a law of enforcement
And the legal persuasion that it had taken away.
So many natural parental rights, it had nurtured a
Generation of untouchables, so visible on that night
That the government's law enforcer raised its hand,
Slammed it down, roaring, "This is not acceptable.
You must pay for the consequences of your actions."

Off to the tower. Throw away the key.
This case is to be reviewed, year unknown!

August 20, 2011
Revised July 23, 2016

Prejudices

When you've got these, you aren't getting on with a true life.
Ensures you're simply consumed in hating for no reason or rhyme.
Wraps you up in a suffocated fear of 100 percent unsupported facts.
Allows minds to be derailed into dismissing logical thinking.
Is a sinister trick creating hate groups full of destruction and lies.
Isn't it time to ditch this bandwagon and get an upgrade in thinking?
What does it matter when, as human beings, we're all the same!

March 8, 2016

The World Is Outta Money

Talk in town seems so gloomy.
People are losing their jobs and their homes daily.
What's the point of talking about a future?
Who should be blamed for all these worries?

When the confusion of it all seems unreal,
Solutions seem based on printing more money!
How do you see a picture in a future with little or no hope?
Surrounded by uncertainty everything can seem impossible.

What is there to hold onto?
What should we do? And how must we try to survive?
When all we knew and loved just disappeared?
Where will we go? How will we trade for food and clothes?

If the world has run outta money!

April 2009
Revised May 7, 2011

Blessings

I'm wishing everyone a new year until they leave,
Full of blessings in which you have continued good health
And the realization of your dreams becomes the reality you start living.

That you have a solid support network that surrounds
You with loving friends, family, but if you have neither of these
That in your times of trouble, then kindness will visit you in your time of need.

That you have the courage to change those things
No longer working for you or bringing you joy or fulfillment
Even whilst feeling the fear and doing it anyway. You know you can!

That happiness is your chief in command even when it feels
Like you are swimming against the tide and that if you have faith,
It is your bedrock anchored in your belief embedded deep in your soul.

Whatever you do, that it's enshrined in blessings full of all that you desire

Each year. Let's keep in touch.

December 31, 2015

MUSICAL WORDS TO FEED THE SOUL

Special Love

Through your eyes, you look around and see love all around you,
And you wonder when will it be just for you.
'Cause there's a longing down deep inside
To find a special someone.

Pre-hook
To find the one who'll be there,
The one who will care,
The one who will stand by my side.

Chorus
So tell me, where did the love go?
When will I find it?
When will I find the love I see all around me?
So tell me, where did the love go?
When will I find it waiting patiently to take me in its arms?
My special love, my special love, my special love.

Keep searching; you will find love
If you open up your mind.
But in your dreams, you don't believe that it will come true,
And the days become years of tears.

Pre-hook
To find the one who'll be there,
The one who will care,
The one who will stand by my side.

Chorus
So tell me, where did the love go?
When will I find it?
When will I find the love I see all around me?
So tell me, where did the love go?
When will I find it waiting patiently to take me in its arms?
My special love, my special love, my special love.

Bridge
Now that I've found you,
It's so amazing.
It feels like it's supposed to,
With the sun in my corner,
And joy's my favorite word,
But the thoughts of losing you make it so hard …
Got to find the one who'll be there by my side.

Chorus x 2
So tell me, where did the love go?
When will I find it?
When will I find the love I see all around me?
Tell me, where did the love go?
When will I find it waiting patiently to take me in its arms?
My special love, special love, my special love.

April 2011

Your Smile

Chorus
Oh, your smile,
Your smile brings warmth when the sun don't shine,
Makes angels dance and drink red wine.
I'll cross the lines into your arms,
For your smile, your smile, your smile makes me lose my mind.

Verse 1
On the nights we sit huddled tight,
Fires burning and dancing real bright,
Chilling to those mellow love sounds of Barry White,
Sipping wine, making promises I know we can't fight.
Then I know that we're all right!

Chorus
Oh, your smile,
Your smile brings warmth when the sun don't shine,
Makes angels dance and drink red wine.
I'll cross the lines into your arms,
For your smile, your smile, your smile makes me lose my mind.

Verse 2
In your arms feels just right.
I feel the warmth of your breath in your smile.
I'm floating in paradise when the time has no sense.
My eyes close. My world is all yours, and we don't fight.
Then I know that we're all right.

Chorus
Oh, your smile,
Your smile brings warmth when the sun don't shine,
Makes angels dance and drink red wine.
I'll cross the lines into your arms,
For your smile, your smile, your smile makes me lose my mind.

Bridge
Everything stands still, and you know it's a dream,
It's an illusion of the mind.
Everything stands still, and you know it ain't real, not even for a while.
Everything stands still, tell how will it be all right.

Chorus x 2
Oh, your smile,
Your smile brings warmth when the sun don't shine,
Makes angels dance and drink red wine.
I'll cross the lines into your arms,
For your smile, your smile, your smile makes me lose my mind.

2012

Friday Night

The boss has gone, and it's Friday night.
We're gonna kick it all back and relax in that vibe.
We're shakin' off all the stress and strains, gonna get with our friends and hang in the groove.
We're riding the subway to town, and we're laughing, talking, getting in that mood.

And when we get there, we're gonna party,
We're gonna party all night.

We're gonna party hard till the break of dawn.
We're gonna party hard till the break of dawn.
We're gonna lose ourselves as we dance till dawn.
We're gonna party hard till the break of dawn.
Yeah …

The room so loud with nowhere to speak, and
Energy is flowing, the DJ's so sound.
There's gonna be no worries about an
Early night 'cause we're here to stay.
It's Friday night, we're gonna shake it up loose on that dance floor tonight.

And when we get there, we're gonna,
We're gonna party all night.
Oh yeah …

Chorus and ad libs
We're gonna party hard till the break of dawn.
   (We're gonna party, we're gonna party, yeah.)
We're gonna party hard till the break of dawn.
   (We're gonna party till the break of dawn.)
We're gonna lose ourselves as we dance till dawn.
   (We're gonna lose our souls, we're gonna dance till dawn.)
We're gonna lose ourselves dancing outta of control.
   (We're gonna party hard till the break of dawn.)
We're gonna party hard till the break of dawn.

It's Friday night. *(x 4)*
It's Friday night.
It's Friday night, gonna dance till dawn.

Yeah, it's Friday night.

May 15, 2010

Let Me Stay

You whisper in my ear.
Your voice sounds so mellow to my heart.
I just wanna be with you.
Forever and a day, you will only be mine
Till the break of dawn.

Pre-hook
If only for tonight, I will be all you want me to be.
If only for tonight, please let me stay.

Chorus
Let me stay forever in your arms.
I wanna stay, oh, wrapped up in your arms.
Please let me stay forever in your arms.
I wanna stay if only for tonight.

Every time you're near,
My pulse becomes so weak. When we're apart,
That I can't live without you.
The days roll on, and the nights become so long;
It feels like eternity.

Pre-hook
If only for tonight, I will be all you want me to be.
If only for tonight, please let me stay.

Chorus
Let me stay forever in your arms.
I wanna stay, oh, wrapped up in your arms.
Please let me stay forever in your arms.
I wanna stay if only for tonight.

Pre-hook x 2
If only for tonight, I will be all you want me to be.
If only for tonight, please let me stay.

Chorus
Let me stay forever in your arms.
I wanna stay, oh, wrapped up in your arms.
Oh, let me stay, baby, stay forever in your arms.
I wanna stay if only for tonight.
Please let me stay, let me stay.

March 17, 2009

Tell Me

As I look into your eyes,
I see the moon and the stars above.
I hear the magic of your voice;
It's printed deep into my heart,
And I know I'm lost in this special world.

Pre-chorus
And I say to myself, oh, what a wonderful feeling
Is this love? That's what I'm feeling. Is this love?

Chorus
Tell me, is this love first thing in the morning
And when I'm holding you so close into the night?
Tell me, is this love when you say I'm always on your mind
And that we'll be together forever in time?
Tell me, is this love? Tell me, is this love?
Oh, is this love?

In my heart, there's no space for another.
Who could make me feel so totally complete!
And even when we're oceans apart and
The emptiness is tearing me apart,
I still see you, and you feel so near.

Pre-chorus
And I say to myself, oh, what a wonderful feeling.
Is this love? That's what I'm feeling. Is this love?

Chorus
Tell me, is this love first thing in the morning
And when I'm holding you so close into the night?
Tell me, is this love when you say I'm always on your mind
And that we'll be together forever in time?
Tell me, is this love? Tell me, is this love?
Oh, is this love?

Bridge
'Cause I know you will never ever leave me
Because our love keeps getting stronger each day, and
You're always there when I need you.
You give me love, sweet love,
And I know you're the only one.

Pre-chorus
And I say to myself, oh, what a wonderful feeling.
Is this love? That's what I'm feeling. Is this love?

Chorus
Tell me, is this love first thing in the morning
And when I'm holding you so close into the night?
Tell me, is this love when you say I'm always on your mind
And that we'll be together forever in time?
Tell me, is this love?

May 7, 2011

Stormy Weather

There's a buzz in town
That says everything's outta control,
People are duckin' and divin',
Trying to keep it all together
So that we can overcome this stormy weather.

Chorus
We gotta hush and be quiet and let it all go away,
And when the sun comes out, we'll know that it's all over,
And everything that we are and everything we do is so
That we can overcome this stormy weather.

We're beaverin' away tryin' to stitch it all together,
Not knowin' what we really wanna do.
We gotta stop this situation, it's truly outta control,
So that we can overcome this stormy weather.

Chorus
We gotta hush and be quiet and let it all go away,
And when the sun comes out, we'll know that it's all over,
And everything that we are and everything we do is so
That we can overcome this stormy weather.

Bridge
And we can fly to the moon and dive the deepest seas,
And we'll watch as the rainbows, they all appear,
'Cause we're still waiting, and we're watching for what's gonna happen!
So that we can overcome this stormy weather.

Chorus
We gotta hush and be quiet and let it all just go away,
And when the sun comes out, we'll know that it's all over,
And everything that we are and everything we do is so
That we can overcome.
We will overcome, yeah, hey,
We will overcome this stormy weather.

May 2009

Friends

Verse 1
It's a license to be open, candid and me.
Your unspoken love is like a magic sent from up above.
That bond that we share has taken us through many a year.
A love that's unspoken, it just keeps on ever strong.

Pre-chorus
It's crossed all the boundaries, and it's running, it's totally free.
It's tearless and fearless, and it's all wrapped up in me.

Chorus
'Cause we are friends,
Friends till the end of time.
We are friends in joy and sorrow we share.
We'll be friends. I'll catch those tears for you.
We are friends no matter what we do.

Verse 2
You're trusted in secrets guarded all times, and
Like a solider, you defend what's on that line.
You see …

Pre-chorus
It's crossed all the boundaries, and it's running, it's totally free.
It's tearless and fearless, and it's all wrapped up in me.

Chorus
'Cause we are friends,
Friends till the end of time.
We are friends in joy and sorrow we share.
We'll be friends. I'll catch those tears for you.
Friends no matter what we do.

Bridge
Demands may be high for you, but you don't turn your back and walk away.
You hold your head with hope in your heart while you say …

Chorus x 2
'Cause we are friends,
Friends till the end of time.
We are friends in joy and sorrow we share.
We'll be friends. I'll catch those tears for you.
Friends no matter what we do.

April 2014

How Could You?

If lovin' you is like a criminal offense,
There ain't nothing left but jail.
If stayin' on the road was so hard in love,
So you drove right into a storm.
You kept me in the dark like a shipwreck
Drifting out, I'm going nowhere.

Pre-chorus
I'm sitting here alone in the darkness,
Watching those shadows of what used to be,
Of what used to be.

Chorus
How could you give our love to
Somebody else?
Wasn't it enough that I loved you?
That you threw it right back at me?
And how could you, how could you do this to me?

Verse
The darkness in my heart has covered my eyes
And crystallized like silver tears.
There's nothing in reserve for a rainy day,
Only the pain of shattered tears,
The jigsaw pieces of my broken life
Are scattered out into the abyss.

Pre-chorus
I'm sitting here alone in the darkness,
Watching those shadows of what used to be,
Of what used to be.

Chorus
How could you give our love to
Somebody else?
Wasn't it enough that I loved you?
That you threw it right back at me?
And how could you, how could you do this to me?

Bridge
Maybe I'm still gonna love you,
Oh, as sad as it may seem.
Or maybe you're gonna love me, baby, but tell me, what will it mean?

Chorus
How could you give our love to
Somebody else?
Wasn't it enough that I loved you?
That you threw it right back at me?
And how could you, how could you do this to me?

Outro
How could, baby, how could you, baby, how could you give our love to someone else?
How could, baby, how could you, baby, how could you give our love to someone else?
How could, baby, how could you, my darling, how could you give our love to someone else?
How could you, how could you do this to me?

September 26, 2011

You Will Be There

When you walked into my life,
It all began to seem so right.
We built a bridge of everlasting steel
That's holding up our hearts as one.
In you I know what love is.
I've seen my life unfold and grow
With a love that's ever intoxicating
And that's ever sincere.

Pre-chorus
You showed how to love you, so I opened up that door.
You showed me how to love you, and I fear it no more.

Chorus x 2
When I need you,
You will be there.
And when I want you,
You will be there.
And if I should fall,
You will catch me;
You will be there.

It feels like a dream, yet it's so real.
Still holding on to forever yours.
You gave me the will, to fly like a butterfly.
I'm reaching out to the stars above.

Pre-chorus
You showed how to love you, so I opened up that door.
You showed me how to love you, and I fear it no more.

Chorus x 2
When I need you,
You will be there.
When I want you,
You will be there.
And if I should fall,
You will catch me;
You will be there.

Tell me, in times of trouble,
Will you shake loose these chains of love,
Or will you leave me so brokenhearted I'm holding my head in my hands?
Or will you be that superhero stepping right and crossing that line?

Chorus x 2
When I need you,
You'll be there.
When I want you,
You'll be there.
And if I should fall,
You will catch me;
You will be there.

March 8, 2012

Distant Love

Everything's drifting away.
There's stillness in the room,
Clouding over my mind,
And the memories of your reflection
Seem to be fading away (*so away*).

Click as the energy floats away.
It's like a candle blown out in the night,
And the atmosphere so tight,
And the darkness takes away all that I had. Are you?

Chorus
My distant love living in a faraway place in my mind?
You'll see the loneliness has covered my eyes,
And as I search in my soul to see,
When will you, are you gonna come back to me (*meee*)?

I'm livin' in an empty space
Where the solitude talks to me all the time,
As sorrowful pulses echo in my mind,
I sit and wait in vain (*in vain*).

The TV's playing away all the time,
And the sound of the voices fill the air.
It breaks down the walls of silence
But still leaves an empty space in my heart. Are you?

Chorus
My distant love living in a faraway place in my mind?
You'll see the loneliness has covered my eyes,
And as I search in my soul to see,
When will you, are you gonna come back to me?

Bridge
The emptiness is painful to see
Unless you're gonna come home to me.
Where I can hear your voice filling the air,
It's gonna take away all this despair.
Oh, cause you're?

Chorus x 2
My distant love living in a faraway place in my mind?
You'll see the loneliness has covered my eyes,
And as I search in my soul to see,
When will you, are you gonna come back to me?

May 25, 2011

TRUE DIRECTIONS
An affiliate of Tarcher Perigee

OUR MISSION

Tarcher Perigee's mission has always been to publish books that contain great ideas. Why? Because:

GREAT LIVES BEGIN WITH GREAT IDEAS

At Tarcher Perigee, we recognize that many talented authors, speakers, educators, and thought-leaders share this mission and deserve to be published – many more than Tarcher Perigee can reasonably publish ourselves. True Directions is ideal for authors and books that increase awareness, raise consciousness, and inspire others to live their ideals and passions.

Like Tarcher Perigee, True Directions books are designed to do three things: inspire, inform, and motivate.

Thus, True Directions is an ideal way for these important voices to bring their messages of hope, healing, and help to the world.

Every book published by True Directions– whether it is non-fiction, memoir, novel, poetry or children's book – continues Tarcher Perigee's mission to publish works that bring positive change in the world. We invite you to join our mission.

For more information, see the True Directions website:

www.iUniverse.com/TrueDirections/SignUp

Be a part of Tarcher Perigee's community to bring positive change in this world! See exclusive author videos, discover new and exciting books, learn about upcoming events, connect with author blogs and websites, and more! www.tarcherbooks.com

TRUE DIRECTIONS
AN AFFILIATE OF TARCHER PERIGEE

Lightning Source UK Ltd.
Milton Keynes UK
UKOW04f2358020917
308452UK00002B/16/P